Killer PENTATONICS

INNOVATIVE AND DIVERSE WAYS OF PLAYING PENTATONIC SCALES IN BLUES, ROCK AND HEAVY METAL

BY DAVE CELENTANO

Cover Art – Eddie Young
Layout & Production – Ron Middlebrook

ISBN 1-57424-113-3
SAN 683-8022

CD Track List

Contents

~ Foreword ~

I didn't want this book to be just another collection of the same old cliché pentatonic licks, so while preparing material for this book I opened my mind (and imagination) to every conceivable possibility the pentatonic scale had.

The licks and ideas included in this volume will give you fresh and diverse approaches to playing the pentatonic scale, hopefully inspiring you to reach for higher levels in your playing.

~ Acknowledgments ~

A special thanks to my wife Kris, Mom and Dad,
Frank Green at D'Angelico Strings and God.

~ Dedication ~

This book is dedicated to the memory of my brother
Douglas Celentano, October 29. 1969 to August 13, 1991

Dave Celentano grew up in Laurel, Maryland where he received invaluable guitar lessons from Marty Friedman. After high school Dave relocated to Southern California to attend G.I.T. in Hollywood. This proved to be the spark that would ignite his motivation and drive to achieve a list of accomplishments. To date he has written seven guitar instruction books and tapes for Centerstream Publishing (distributed by Hal Leonard Publishing): 'The Magic Touch', 'Flying Fingers', 'Rock Licks', 'Speed Metal', 'The Art of Transcribing', 'Monster Scales and Modes' and his latest effort 'Killer Pentatonic's'. He's also transcribed many books for Hal Leonard: Alice in Chains 'Facelift', Bon Jovi 'New Jersey', Vixen 'Rev it Up', Warrant 'D.R.F.S.R.', and Armored Saint 'Symbol of Salvation'. Star Licks commissioned him to do several guitar instructional videos including 'Randy Rhoads Style', 'Eric Clapton Style', 'Guitar Tricks', 'Bon Jovi', 'Aerosmith' and 'Scorpions'.

Currently Dave's teaching guitar at Waltrip's Music in Arcadia, California, Grayson's Tunetown in Montrose, California and Gard's Music in Glendora, California. He's also performing clinics for D'Angelico strings at music stores all over the west coast.

TIPS ON PRACTICING

— Practice with a metronome.
— Start out playing slowly and gradually build up speed. No matter how fast you can play, if it sounds sloppy it will always sound amateurish.
— Strive to make all your notes sound even and clear. Your playing shouldn't sound choppy or like a sputtering engine.
— If you feel your hand cramping up or experience any pain, take a break. It's great to practice a lot, but don't overdo it if there's pain. Watch out for the wide stretch licks.

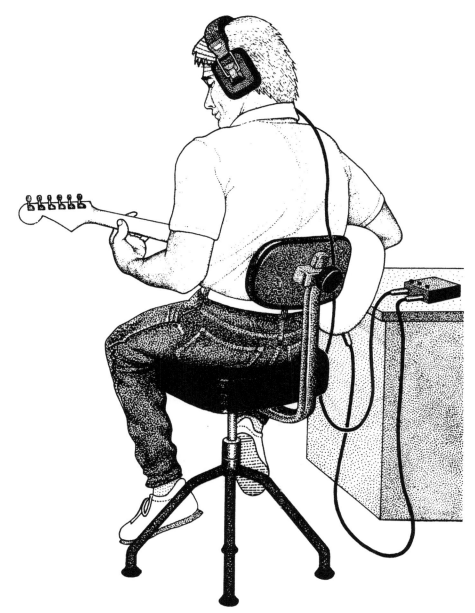

PENTATONIC SCALE
-BACKGROUND AND THEORY-

With the birth of three chord rock and roll in the 50's came the need for a simple scale that could be easily played and yet still satisfy the audience's ear with the 'right notes'. The pentatonic scale (often dubbed the 'blues scale') became the scale of choice.

The name 'pentatonic' is derived from two words; penta meaning five in Greek and tonic meaning tone. Hence a five tone scale.

Although the pentatonic scale has increased in popularity over the last few decades with the acceptance of rock and roll and heavy metal, it's been used for hundreds of years in eastern music (Japanese and Chinese).

There's two types of pentatonic scales to learn: major pentatonic and minor pentatonic. We'll begin with the major pentatonic scale in the key of 'A', since 'A' is one of the most popular keys to play in on the guitar.

Major Pentatonic

"A" major pentatonic contains these notes:

	A	B	C#	E	F#
scale degrees -	1 (root)	2	3	5	6

Notice there's only five notes. You could think of major pentatonic as a major scale missing the 4th and 7th scale degrees.

Here's what 'A' major pentatonic looks like on your guitar neck:

A major Pentatonic

Ex.1

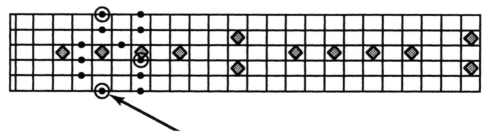

Note: The circled dots are the A's, the root of the scale.

6

Now if you're scratching your head, wondering why you just played <u>twelve</u> notes and a minute ago you learned that the pentatonic scale has <u>five</u> notes, here's why:

The pentatonic scale has five <u>different</u> notes. The remaining notes are just the five notes repeated one octave higher and then a second octave higher until you run out of strings.

Every scale can be broken down into five separate finger patterns covering the entire finger board. Below are those patterns for A major pentatonic:

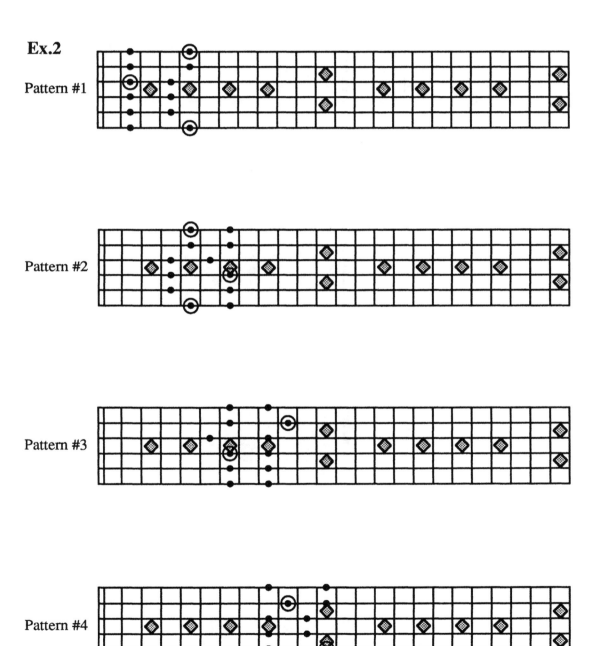

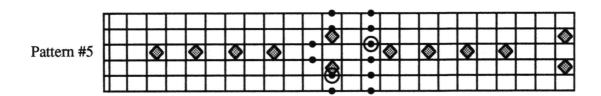

Pattern #5

Here are all the notes in A major pentatonic covering the entire finger board:

Ex.3

Minor Pentatonic

The minor pentatonic is the second type of pentatonic scale to learn. Again, I'll use the key of 'A' for describing this scale. The notes in A minor pentatonic are:

	A	C	D	E	G
scale degrees	1	b3	4	5	b7
	(root)				

The minor pentatonic could be thought of as a natural minor scale missing the 2nd and 6th scale degrees. A minor pentatonic looks like this on your guitar neck:

Ex.4

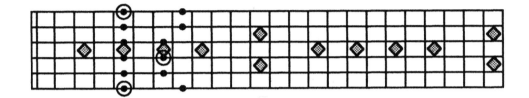

Just like the major pentatonic, the minor pentatonic scale can be broken down into five separate finger patterns. Here are the five patterns for A minor pentatonic:

Ex.5

Pattern #1

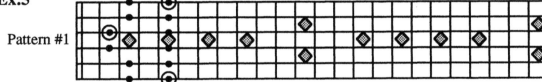

Pattern #2

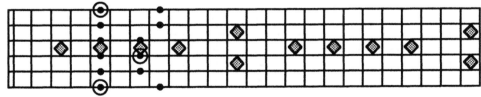

Pattern #3

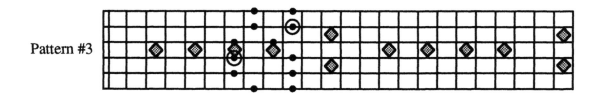

Pattern #4

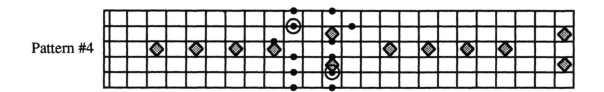

Pattern #5

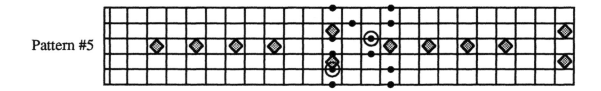

> **Memorize all five patterns! This is the first step to being able to solo effortlessly all over the fretboard.**

Here are all the notes in A minor pentatonic covering the entire finger board;

Ex.6

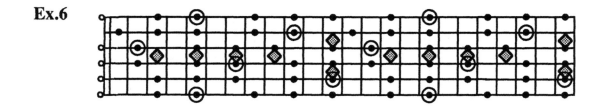

Did you notice that the major and minor pentatonic scales both use the exact same five patterns? The only difference is which note serves as the root.

The major and minor pentatonic scales are not exclusive of each other. Often times a guitarist will combine both in the same solo.

Example: Play 'A' minor pentatonic and then switch to 'A' major pentatonic, playing both scales over an A7 chord.

Here's a little trick to easily switch from minor to major pentatonic:

Play the root position pattern (#2, 5th fret) in A minor pentatonic. Next, slide that same pattern back <u>three</u> frets to begin on F# (2nd fret) and play the scale here. You are now playing in A major pentatonic.

Guitarists in all styles of music use this trick all the time, like Gary Rossington and Allen Collins from Lynyrd Skynyrd, the Allman Brothers, Eric Clapton, Frank Gambale and Larry Carlton.

Remember this rule of thumb for combining major and minor pentatonic: When you're soloing using any of the five finger patterns with the minor pentatonic scale move the same pattern you're using down <u>three</u> frets and this yields a major-ish, country sound. See how simple it is!

By examining the diagrams of the entire scales in Examples 3 and 6 you'll notice that the notes diagrammed on the finger board past pattern #5 are simply duplications of patterns 1, 2, 3 and part of 4, played one octave higher. To play pattern #1 and octave higher, simply move it up the neck <u>12</u> frets. Repeat this process for patterns 2, 3 and 4.

Note: For more theory on pentatonic scales and many other scales, check out my book "Monster Scales and Modes," published by Centerstream Publishing.

PLAYING THE PENTATONIC SCALE IN OTHER KEYS

Now you're able to play major and minor pentatonic in the Key of A, but what about other keys? Well, here's how to do it:

First, start with the root position pattern (#2) beginning with A at the fifth fret (this works with both major and minor scales). Next, let's say we're going to play in the key of A#. Since A# is only one fret up from A, we'll move the root position pattern (#2) up one fret to begin at the sixth fret. All the other patterns will also be moved up one fret each to play in the key of A#.

Now try the key of C. C is three frets higher than A, so move the root position pattern up three frets to begin at the 8th fret. Move the other four patterns up three frets also.

You can use this process to play in all keys, but first you must know the names of all the notes on the low 'E' string (6th string). Below is a neck diagram with all the notes on the low 'E' string:

Ex.7

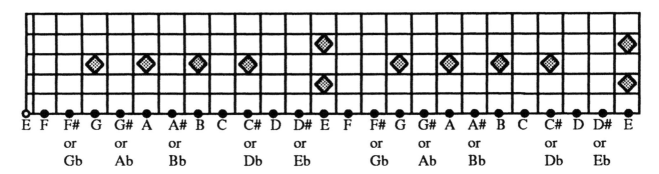

Once you know the names of all the notes on the low "E" string you can begin to play the pentatonic scales in any key, just follow the process described above.

RELATIVE MAJOR AND MINOR

Every major pentatonic scale has a 'relative minor' scale within it. And likewise every minor pentatonic scale has a 'relative major' scale contained within it.

Example - C major pentatonic contains the notes C D E G A. The 'relative minor' scale always starts 3 frets in back of the root for the major pentatonic. Three frets back from C is A, so A minor pentatonic is the 'relative minor' to C major. A minor pentatonic contains the notes A C D E G. Notice that both scales contain the same notes. The only difference is C major pentatonic begins on 'C' and A minor pentatonic beings on 'A'. In other words two different names for one scale.

This means you can play A minor pentatonic over and A minor chord and a C major chord. You can also play A minor pentatonic over a rhythm that is in the key of A minor or C major.

Below is a chart of all the major pentatonic scales along with the corresponding 'relative minor' scales:

Major Pentatonic		Relative Minor Pentatonic
C major	—	A minor
C# or Db major	—	A# or Bb minor
D major	—	B minor
Eb major	—	C minor
E major	—	C# minor
F major	—	D minor
F# or Gb major	—	D# or Eb minor
G major	—	E minor
Ab major	—	F minor
A major	—	F# minor
Bb major	—	G minor
B major	—	G# minor

SINGLE PATTERN LICKS

The licks in this section are written and played in pattern #2 of A minor pentatonic (same as C major pentatonic). Experiment by playing these licks in other keys and patterns as well.

Alternate pick everything unless otherwise notated

(Down, up, down, up, etc.)!

Example 8 thru 11 are licks based on a repeating motif. This 'repetitive' concept was used extensively in the 70's by the likes of Ace Frehley (Kiss), Allen Collins and Gary Rossington (Lynyrd Skynyrd) and Jimmy Page.

In example 8 bar your index finger across the 1st and 2nd strings (5th fret), so that your finger won't have to keep jumping back and forth between strings.

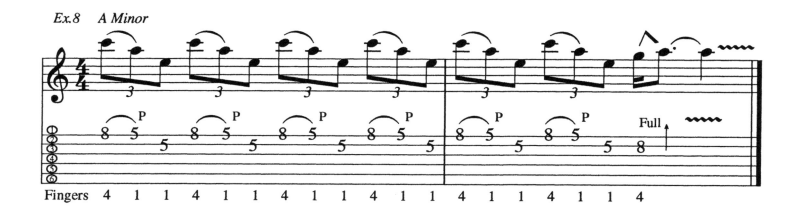

Ex.9 A Minor

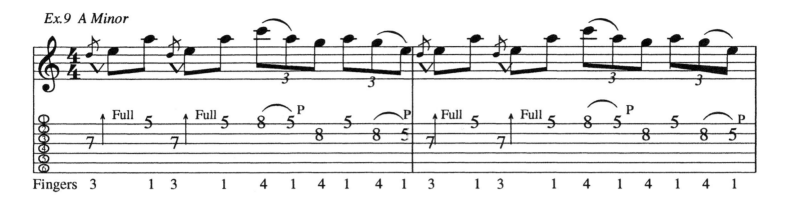

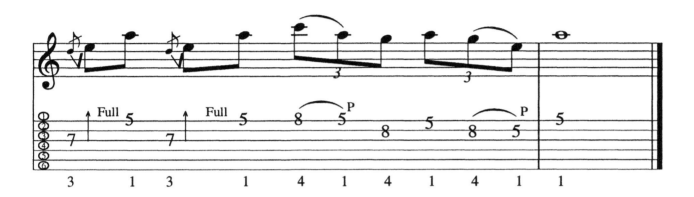

For example 10 bar your 3rd finger across the 3rd and 4th strings at the seventh fret on beats two and four.

Ex.10 A Minor

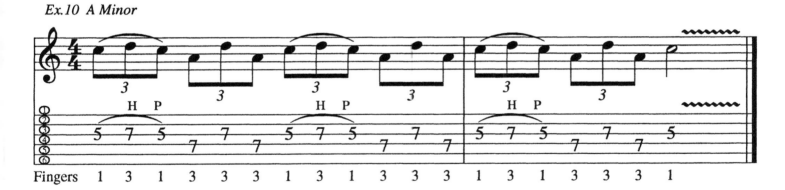

Ex.11 A Minor

Example 12 is an idea using triplets (groups of 3's) and pull-offs.

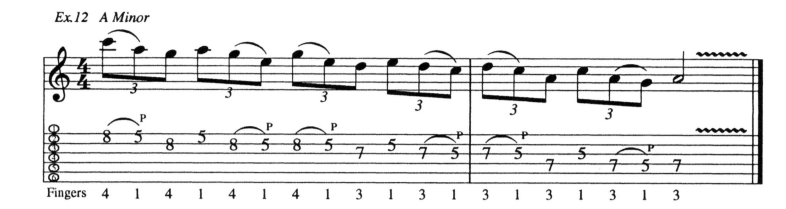

This next lick is similar to example 12, but this one ascends.

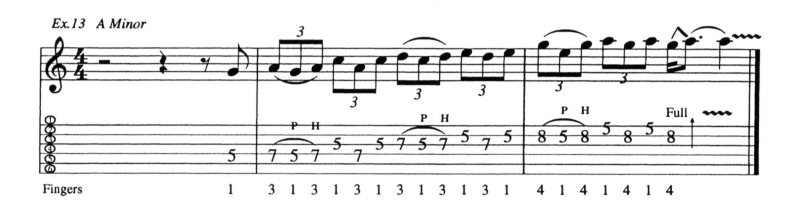

Example 14 is a modern sounding lick using 'sweep picking'. This technique involves a series of consecutive downstrokes followed by a series of consecutive up strokes. Yngwie Malmsteen and Frank Gambale use sweep picking often in their solos.

A detailed look at sweep picking can be found in my book 'Flying Fingers', published by Centerstream Publishing.

For your convenience I've included arrows above the notes indicating which direction to pick each note. Again, bar your fingers across the strings played consecutively on the same fret.

Ex.14 A Minor

Fingers   1 1 1 3 3 4   1 1 1 3 3 3   1 1 1 4 3 3   1 1 1 4 4 3   1

Remember, these licks can also be played over
a 'C major' chord, which is the relative major
to A minor.

17

DOUBLE STOPS

The next three examples use 'double stops'. A double stop is the playing of two notes at the same time. To play the double stops in example 15 bar your index finger across the 1st and 2nd strings at the 5th fret and pick with down strokes. This lick has a Chuck Berry-ish flavor.

Ex.15   A Minor

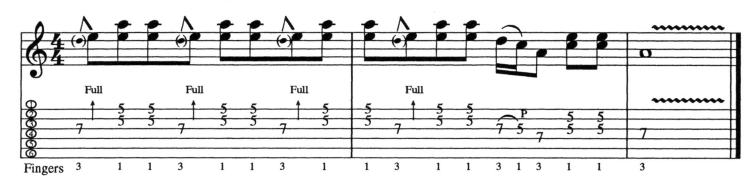

Example 16 and 17 use double stops to produce a country/southern rock sound. These two licks are very typical of Lynyrd Skynyrd and the Allman Brothers.

Ex.16   C Major

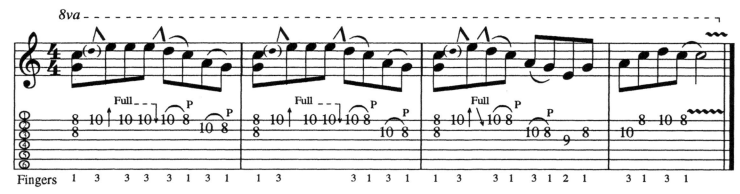

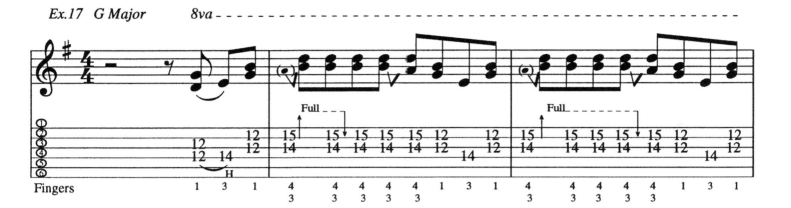

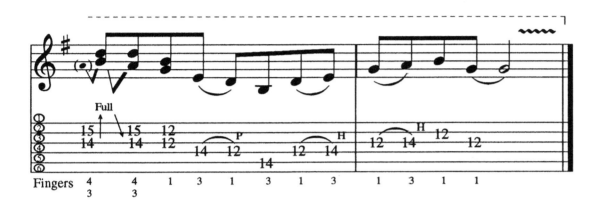

Fingers

CONNECTING THE PATTERNS

Once you can solo comfortably in one pattern the next logical step is to begin connecting the different patterns. Your goal should be to play smoothly from one pattern to the next.

The following collection of licks will introduce your fingers to ideas created by connecting some of the patterns. Example 18 is a rapid ascending lick using triplets in the key of A minor.

Ex.18 A Minor

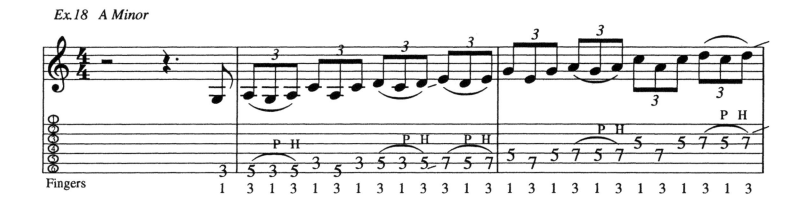

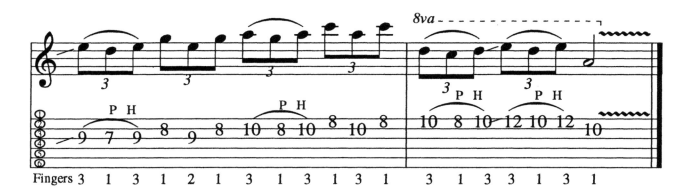

At this point we'll change keys to E minor (relative major is G) for the next two examples.

Example 20 is heavily influenced by the late Randy Rhoads. He often used 'tremolo picking' to create fast lines. Tremolo picking is the rapid repetition of a single note. This technique can also be found in Eddie Van Halen guitar solo 'Eruption'. **ALTERNATE PICK EVERY NOTE!**

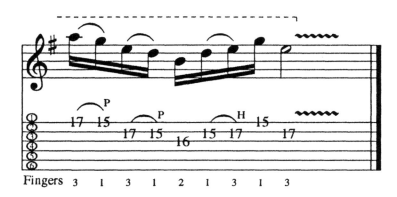

A common way of playing major and minor scales is to organize the patterns so there are 3 notes per string. For example 21 I've laid out A minor pentatonic with 3 notes per string. By setting up the pentatonic scale in this fashion you increase its range by more than one additional octave, plus it looks cool to see your fingers rapidly ascending up the neck. This lick also sounds great descending.

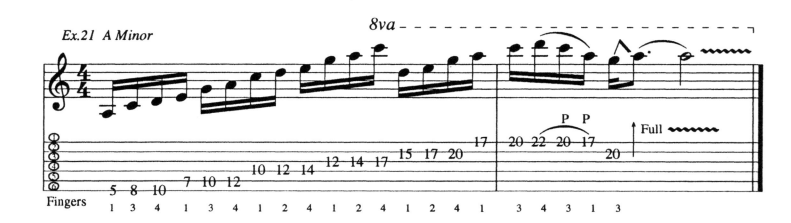

Now figure out what the remaining four patterns would be like using 3 notes per string.

BLUES WITH PENTATONICS

Displayed in this section are two blues solos which show again how versatile the pentatonic scale is. Both solos are played over a 12 bar blues chord progression in the key of A. The 12 bar blues is fun to solo over with pentatonics because every note sounds good nearly all the time. Here's the basic structure for the 12 bar blues in A:

```
||:     I  /   IV /   I  /   I  /
      A7 /   D7 /  A7 /   A7 /


       IV /   IV /   I  /   I  /
      D7 /   D7 /  A7 /   A7 /


       V  /   IV /   I  /   V        :||
      E7 /   D7 /  A7 /   E7
```

Notice the repeat signs at the beginning and end of the progression. This means to keep repeating it over and over.

The first solo (Ex. 22) is a slow blues. The nature of the slow blues allows you to put much feeling into each note. Check it out.

23

Ex.22
Slow swing feel 69 b.p.m.

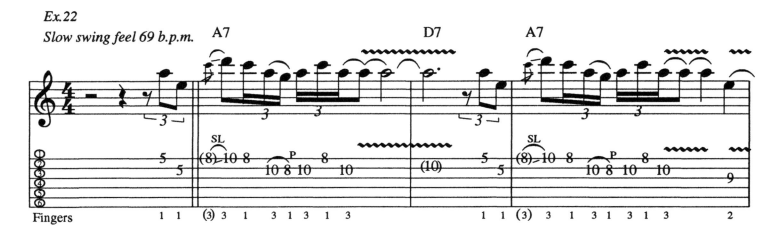

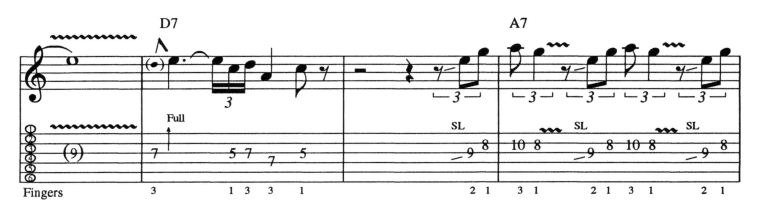

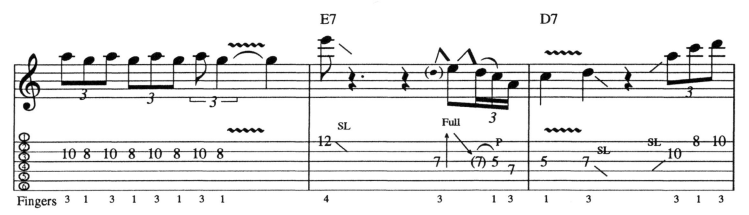

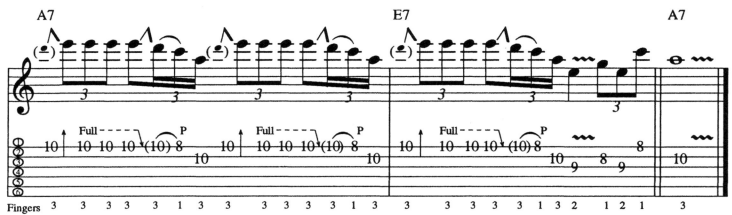

Ex.23

Shuffle feel   112 b.p.m.

The second blues solo is faster and more up beat.

25

EXTENDED PATTERNS

Alan Holdsworth was one of the first to use the 'extended patterns'. Today many guitarists use this concept like Marty Friedman (Megadeth), Steve Vai and Eddie Van Halen. The idea is simple, but very effective. Here's how it works: combine two adjacent patterns, for instance patterns 2 and 3, and play it as one giant three note per string scale.

Diagrammed below are all 5 'extended patterns' in A minor:

Ex. 24

Pattern 1 & 2

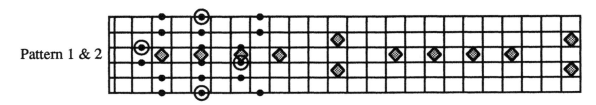

Pattern 2 & 3

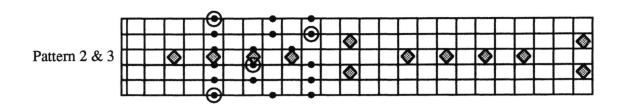

Pattern 3 & 4

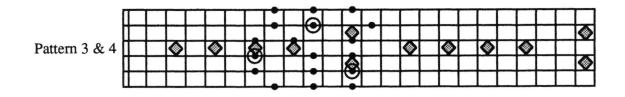

Pattern 4 & 5

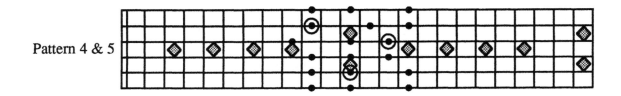

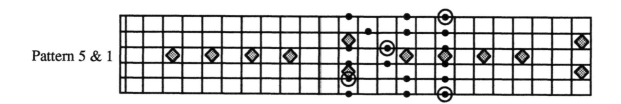

Pattern 5 & 1

Notice the many doubled notes occurring in each pattern. This unique quality gives the extended patterns their own sound.

I love the ultra-modern sounds the extended patterns produce and I believe you will too! Let's move on.

The licks in this section involve some stretching, so I've put all the examples in the key of E minor so newcomers to this concept can play the licks comfortably.

WARNING: If you experience any pain or cramps while attempting the licks in this section, please take a break and let your hand relax for a few minutes.

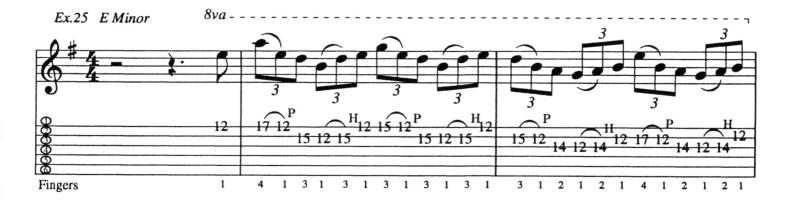

Ex.26   E Minor

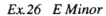

Examples 27 thru 33 take on a different approach. They involve playing the pentatonics in groups of threes, fours, fives and sixs by using the 'extended patterns'. I hear a lot of these ideas in Paul Gilbert's (Mr. Big and Racer X) and Eric Johnson's playing.

Ex.27   E Minor

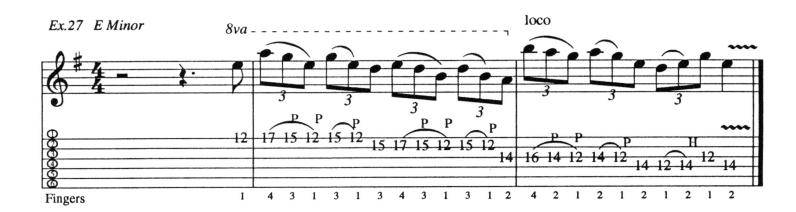

28

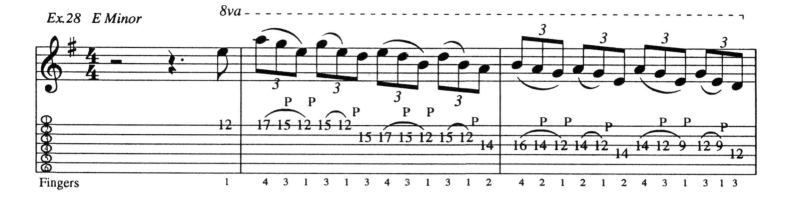

Ex.28 E Minor

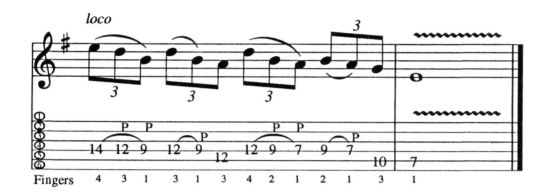

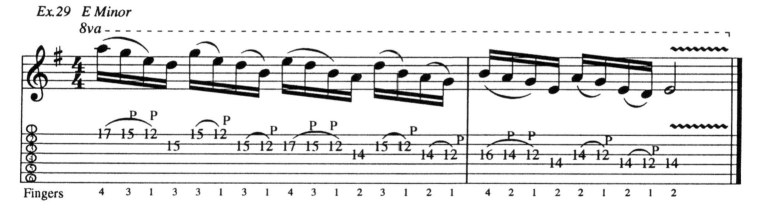

Ex.29 E Minor

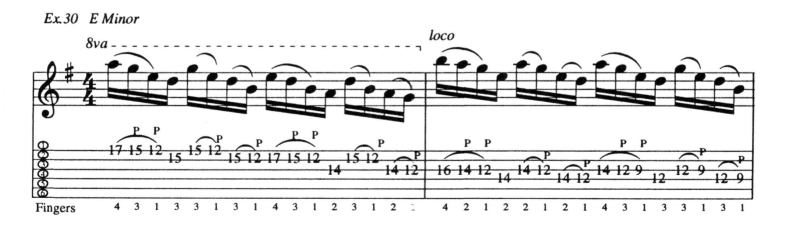

Ex.30 E Minor

Ex.31 E Minor

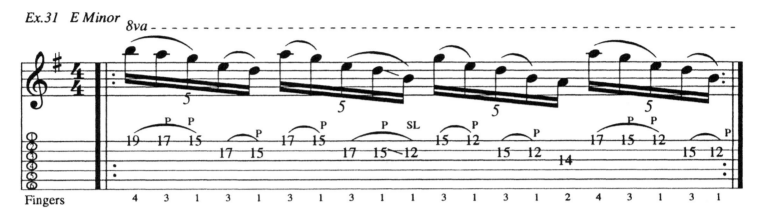

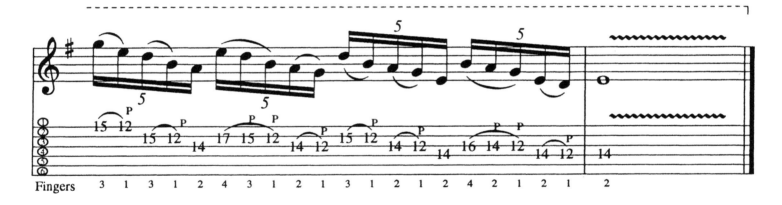

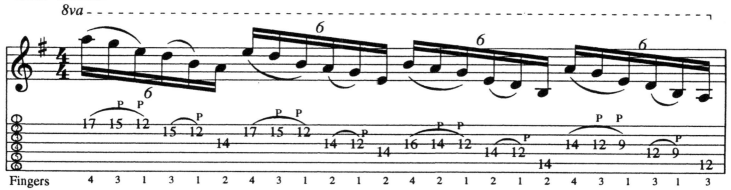

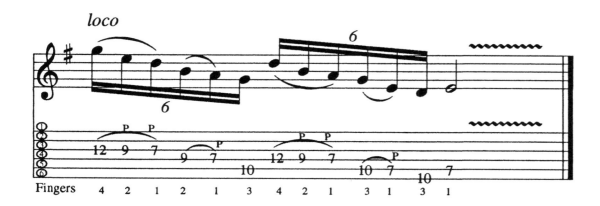

loco

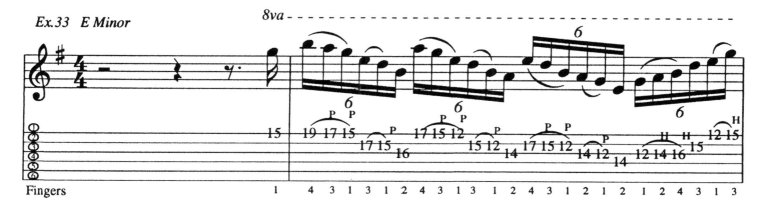

Ex.33   E Minor

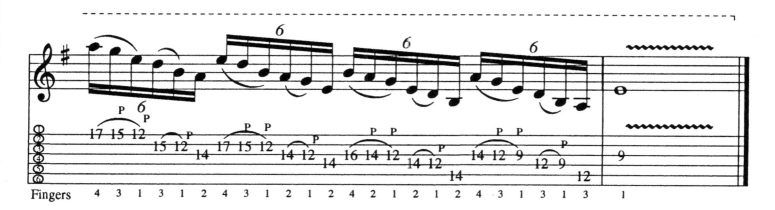

Here's an interesting idea connecting three scale patterns in E minor. The end of this lick is based out of an extended pattern in the same key.

Ex.34 E Minor

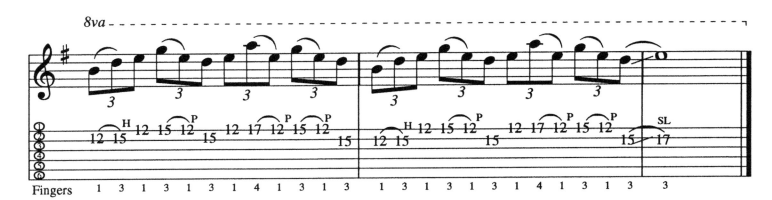

The fingering in this next lick is designed to facilitate speed. It presents an unusual fingering for the otherwise simple pentatonic scale.

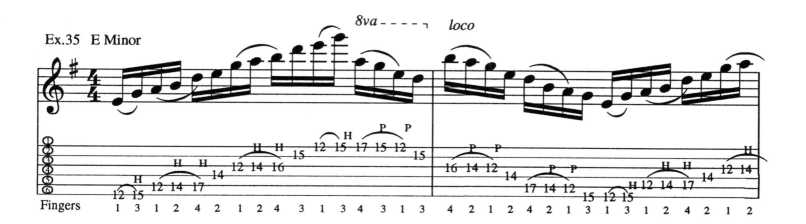

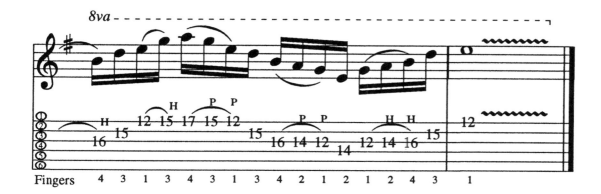

Now we'll try combining a series of ideas to create one big 'monster' lick. Keep in mind to play every note slowly and evenly while learning the lick, then gradually increase your speed. Notice the chord changes above each bar (E min.7 and A7). Record yourself playing these chords then rewind the tape and play example 36 over the chords.

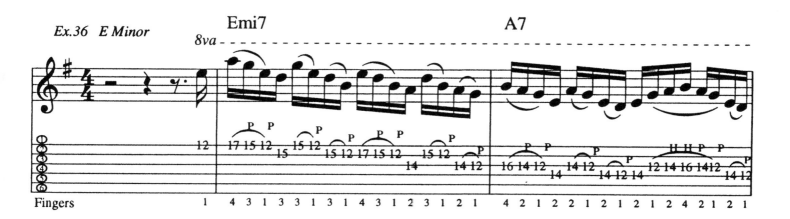

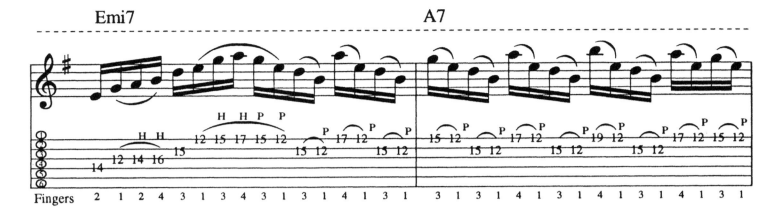

Here's another combination of ideas to create a monster size lick. This lick is influenced heavily by Joe Satriani's burning speed and finesse. Play this lick over E minor and G major chords.

Ex.37 E. Minor

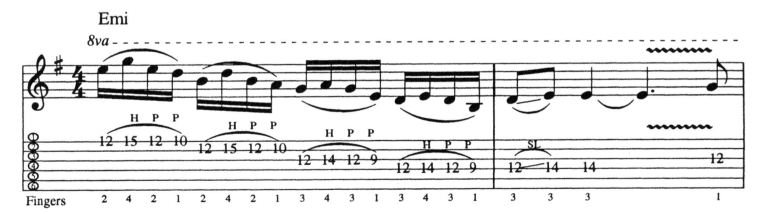

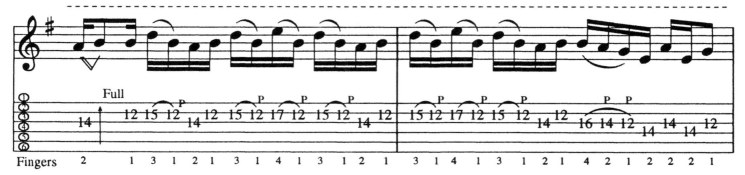

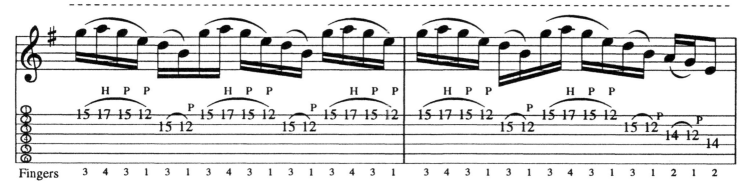

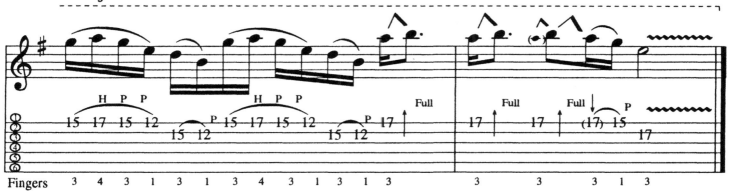

Example 38 is a full solo incorporating many of the ideas previously discussed.
Play this solo over A minor and D major chords.

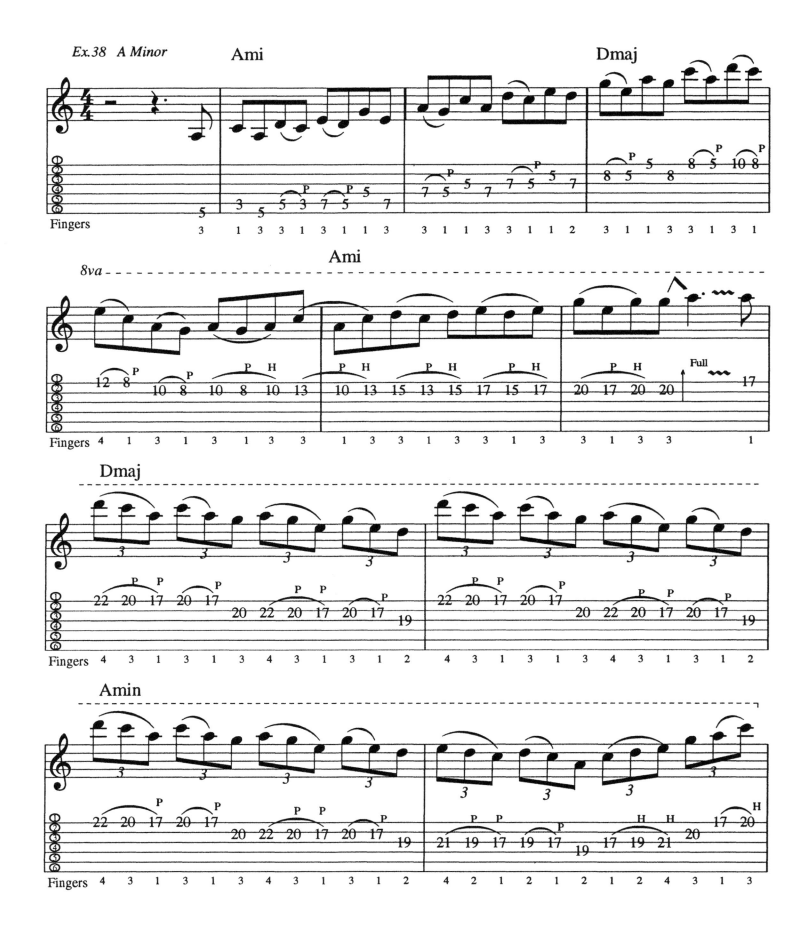

Ex.38 cont.....

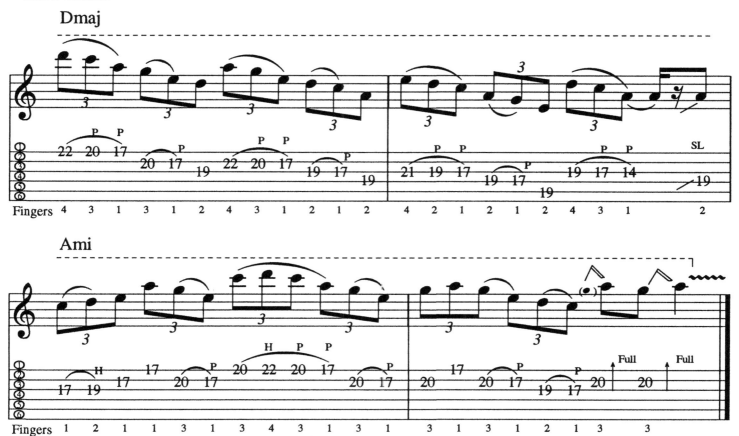

Dmaj

Ami

Once you feel comfortable with these licks, try playing them in other keys as well.

ARPEGGIOS IN PENTATONICS

Many guitarists use arpeggios in their solos. Eddie Van Halen taps arpeggios in 'Eruption' and Randy Rhoads used them at the beginning of his solo in 'Mr. Crowley', but by far the most explicit use of arpeggios is in the guitar solo work of Yngwie Malmsteen.

An arpeggio is the consecutive playing of the notes of any given chord. Contained within the notes of the pentatonic scale are two different arpeggios; major and minor. Assume you're in the key of A minor pentatonic (same as C major pentatonic, the relative major). There is an A minor arpeggio (the notes are A, C, E) and C major arpeggio (the notes are C, E, G) within this scale. So as you're soloing in A minor with your artillery of licks you can play A minor and C major arpeggios.

The examples in this section present a wide variety of arpeggiated licks. Try playing the ideas in other keys as well. Since we've been working with E minor pentatonic a lot in this book, you may want to know that the corresponding arpeggios for this key would be E minor and G major.

Most of the arpeggios in this section will be derived from A minor pentatonic. The first few ideas showcase four variations of the A minor and C major arpeggios using sweep picking. Remember, sweep picking is the use of consecutive downstrokes followed by consecutive upstrokes. The arrows above the notes indicate which direction to pick each note (down, down, down, etc. or up, up, up, etc.).

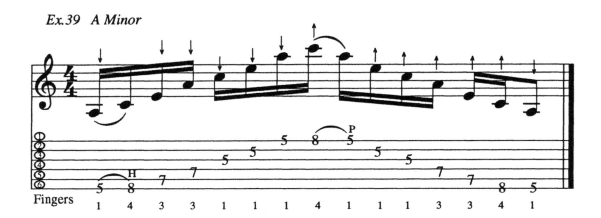

Ex.39 A Minor

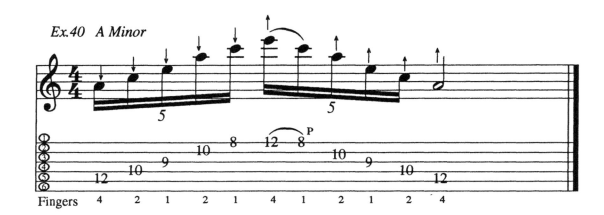

Ex.40 A Minor

Ex.41 A Minor

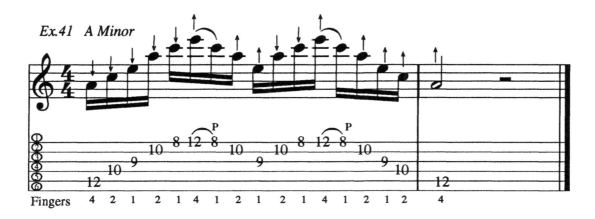

| Fingers | 4 | 2 | 1 | 2 | 1 | 4 | 1 | 2 | 1 | 2 | 1 | 4 | 1 | 2 | 1 | 2 | | 4 |

Ex.42 A Minor

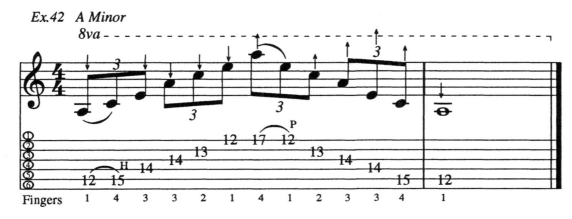

| Fingers | 1 | 4 | 3 | 3 | 2 | 1 | 4 | 1 | 2 | 3 | 3 | 4 | | 1 |

Ex.43 C Major

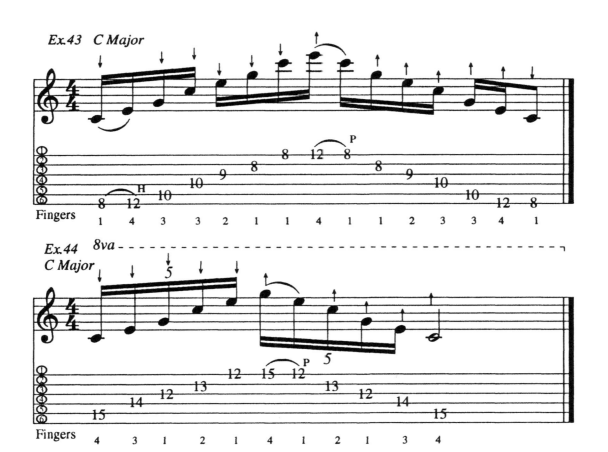

| Fingers | 1 | 4 | 3 | 3 | 2 | 1 | 1 | 4 | 1 | 1 | 2 | 3 | 3 | 4 | 1 |

Ex.44 *C Major*

| Fingers | 4 | 3 | 1 | 2 | 1 | 4 | 1 | 2 | 1 | 3 | 4 |

The next two arpeggiated examples will incorporate string skipping. Nuno Bettencourt (Extreme) and Paul Gilbert (Mr. Big) both use string skipping. Practice these slowly, making the transition between the 3rd and 1st strings smooth and even.

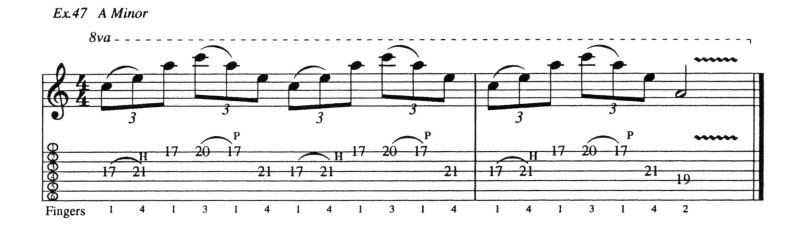

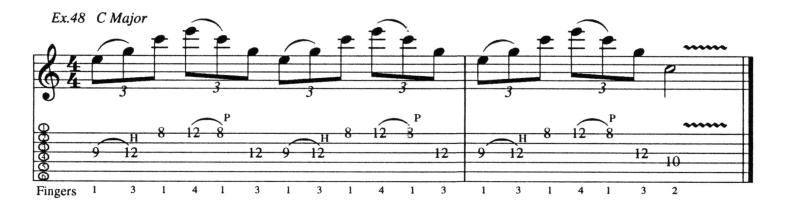

Ex.48 C Major

By combining the notes of the A minor chord (A, C, E) and the C major chord (C, E, G) you have an A minor 7th chord (A, C, E, G). Since A minor 7th has four _different_ notes it lends itself to being played diagonally across the fretboard.

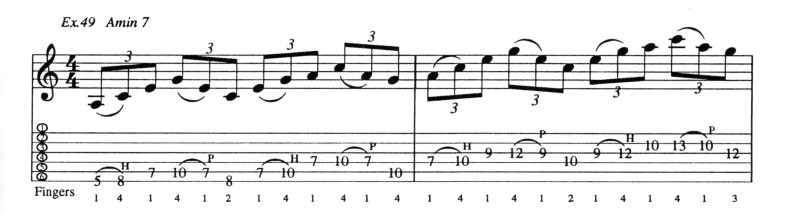

Ex.49 Amin 7

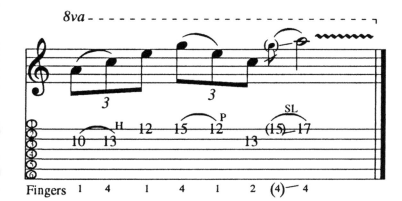

41

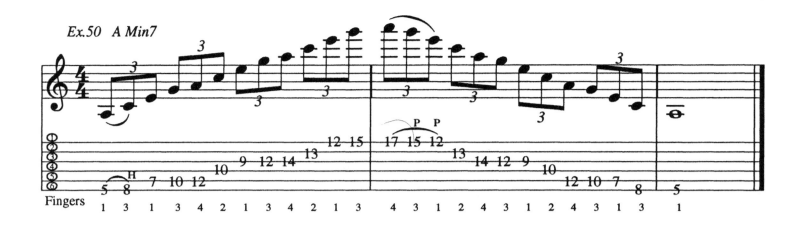

Ex.50 A Min7

Now check out an E minor 7th arpeggio (E, G, B, D). This one involves a stretch from the 12th to the 19th frets! Ouch! The first half of this lick you'll want to sweep pick, so watch the arrows.

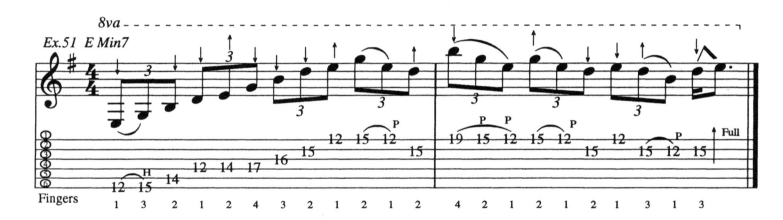

Ex.51 E Min7

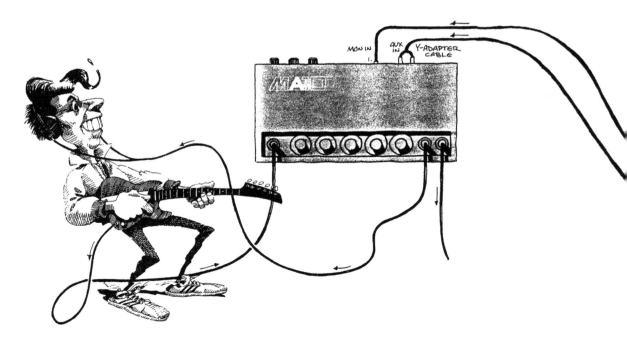

TAPPING WITH PENTATONICS

This section takes us even deeper into the realm of pentatonics by adding the right hand fingers to tap with. If you've never tapped before or you're a novice, don't fear because these tapping licks start with the easiest and gradually build up to the more difficult.

Example 52 features an ascending lick reminiscent of Eddie Van Halen, with some cool string bending at the end. Use your left hand fingers to help bend the strings up when you're bending and tapping at the same time (2nd bar, 2nd beat and 3rd bar, 1st beat).

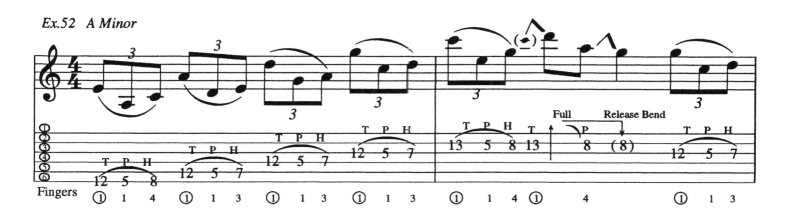

Ex.52 A Minor

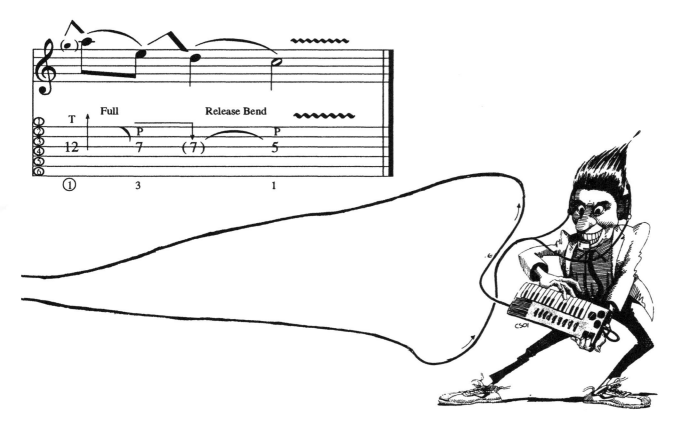

Steve Vai's innovative style inspired the next two tapping licks. They utilize the extended patterns discussed earlier in this book.

Ex.53   E Minor

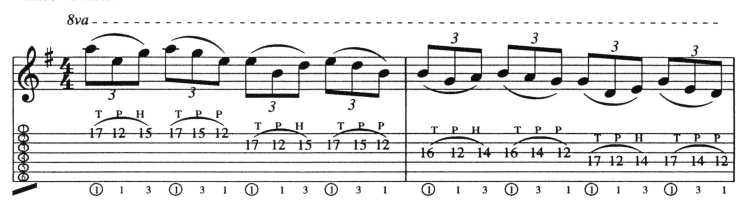

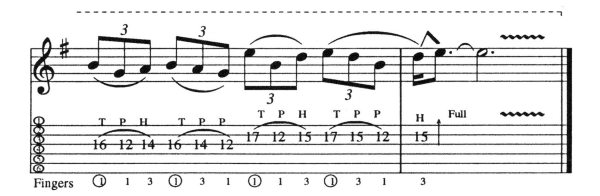

Ex.54   E Minor

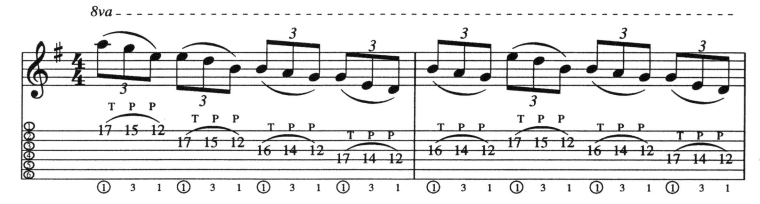

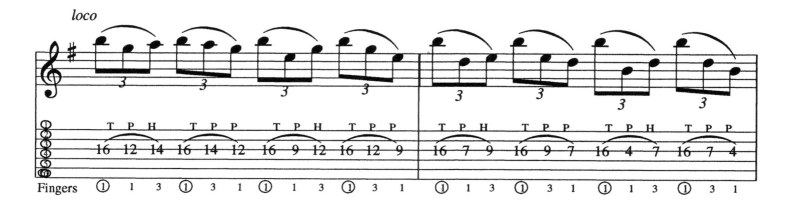

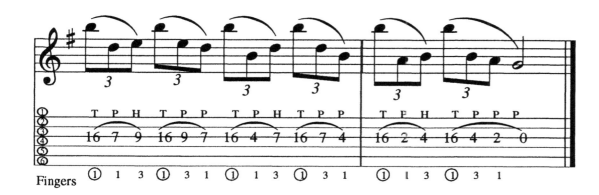

Tapping adapts well to 'linear playing', which is playing up and down the neck on one or two strings. Example 55 demonstrates linear playing on the 2nd string in A minor.

Ex.55   A Minor

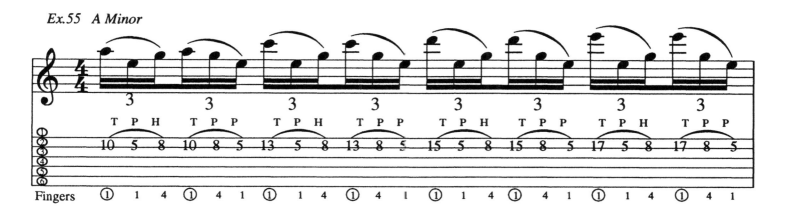

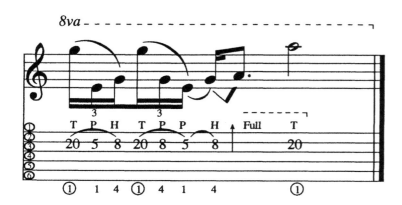

This next lick uses what I call 'double taps'. It involves tapping a note with your right hand and pulling off, then hammering on the same note with your left hand and pulling off. This lick really flies, but to keep your fingers from hitting each other try this little trick:

After tapping the note with your right hand, pull off in an upward direction (towards the ceiling), then hammer on the same note with your left hand and pull off in a downward direction (towards the floor). Practice this motion very slow and gradually get faster.

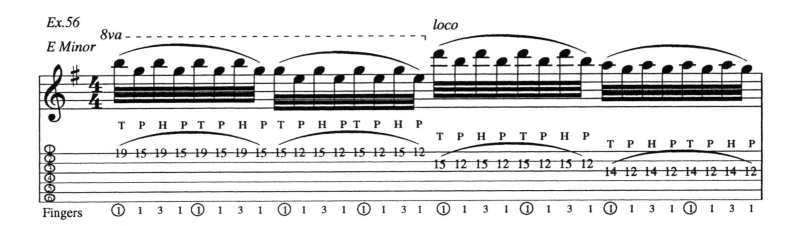

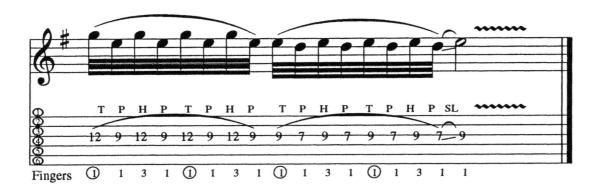

Here's still another idea with the extended patterns.

Ex. 57

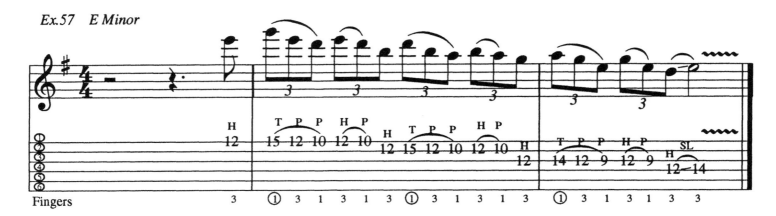

46

Example 58 features 'octave tapping'. All you do is tap a note high on the neck, then pull off to the note 12 frets lower (one octave lower) on the same string. Nuno Bettencourt (Extreme) has experimented with this technique in the past. This technique gives the illusion of using a harmonizer.

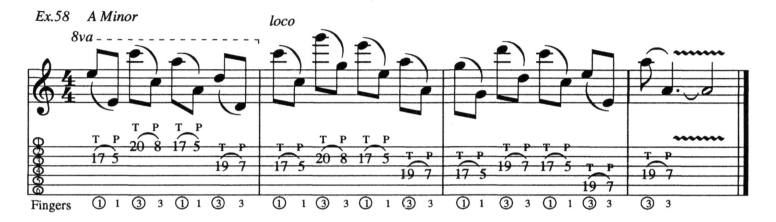

Next is a variation of octave tapping.

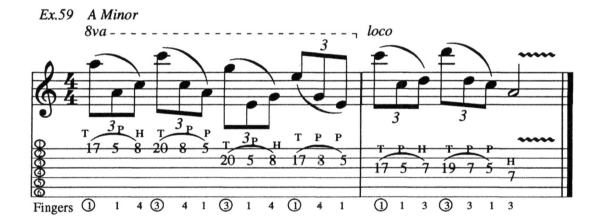

CONCLUSION

As you can see, the pentatonic scale has numerous applications. With a little imagination and experimenting I'm sure you can discover many more licks and tricks lurking in the dephs of the pentatonic scale.

Dave Celentano

For free information on all Dave Celentano's books and tapes write to:

Flying Fingers Productions
P. O. Box 1994
Arcadia, CA 91077-1994

More Great Guitar Books from Centerstream...